EXCEL
VBA

*Basic Beginners Guide to
Learn Excel VBA to Get started*

William Collins

Table of Contents

Introduction

Firstly, I want to say a heartfelt thank you for taking the time to read this book, *Excel VBA*. Also, I want it known that you should be proud of yourself for taking the time to learn something new.

Within this book's contents are some pathways and strategies on how to begin understanding the basics of Visual Basic for Applications. It is here to assist you in learning Visual Basic for Applications from scratch or perhaps even expanding upon your knowledge of writing in Visual Basics for Applications. Visual Basic for Applications is used to create User Defined Functions (UDFs). A User Defined Function is a function that the program user inputs into the program themselves.

Though it is commonly believed that most features (functions) are already coded into the programs that you use, that simply isn't true. By applying Visual Basic for Applications to create new User Defined Functions, you can code your way through the Microsoft Excel program and have an assortment of functions that are key to you. Not only within the Excel spreadsheet, but it can even interact with different parts of the Excel program. Who would not like to create a form to get people's opinions and have that form automatically place their information neatly on a spreadsheet?

Before jumping into learning about Visual Basic for Applications, a little bit of a rundown on the history of Visual Basics for Applications is needed. During the 1960s, not many people outside of the fields of Mathematics and Sciences had much of a purpose for using them back then. That is, until two Dartmouth college students wanted to make it easier for others to be able to use computers as well. Their names are John G. Kemeny and Thomas E. Kurtz, and they developed and launched what we now call BASICs all the way back in May of 1964. Just to give you a visual the minicomputer wasn't made and sold until 1965, and even then, it was not exactly mini.

Going clockwise from top left we have an early computer, Floppy disks, a computer workstation for a business and a minicomputer.

Bonus Computer Trivia: Back in the 1960's Hewlett and Packard and IBM were the major front runners for computers. The first computers that were ever made could fill an entire room, some had to be turned on and off to switch between programs, and the programs were on floppy discs that were actually floppy! The first personal computers were made in 1965 and had only a few programs for owners to use, its processing power was on par with today's graphing calculator.

Before moving on to the rest of the book, I wanted to take the opportunity again and thank you for taking the time to read this and that I hope you enjoy the lessons within it!

Chapter 1

Basics of Visual Basics for Applications

So, Just What Is BASIC?

BASIC is one of the base computer languages; it's an acronym for Beginner's All-purpose Symbolic Instruction Code. Back in the day, programming for computers was more complex before this. Back then, Binary Coding is one of the coding methods that were in use.

Binary is coding written in zeros and ones, think writing a sentence only with I and S with spaces between each letter; it would be one long line of code. BASIC allows you to use keywords and phrases to shorten that coding. Do you know that word Syntax? You probably recognize it but, for the life of you have the idea of what the word means in your brain but, it's probably not quite as fancy as you think. The syntax is how you combine words together to make sentences make sense. Even when you are typing up code, you are using computer syntax to communicate with your computer.

But moving on, BASIC was made by Kemeny and Kurtz, to make it easier for the average person to use a computer. Though they had made BASIC for everyone, it found its own special niche in the small business field. It allowed local business owners to be able to implement specified functions to assist with their everyday needs, from sales to inventory.

BASIC later expanded from there to give us all types of computer languages like COMAL, VisualBasic.net, Xojo, GRASS, RING and Visual Basic for Applications. Also, VBA wasn't always VBA; it started off as Visual, then changed to Visual Basic, then evolved into the Visual Basics for Applications that we use today. It has also implemented into a lot of Microsoft's programming as you can use Visual Basics for Applications in most of the Microsoft programs.

An Explanation Behind How Visual Basics for Applications Works

How does Visual Basics for Applications work? Visual Basics for Applications works by allowing users to implement their own programming codes. Those lines of codes allow for different functions to be performed, even something as simple as creating a message box; it can be programmed to pop up whenever you open a specific spreadsheet or workbook. The message can be to remind you that you need to update a specific item every time. It could even track this year's sales to calculate the goals for next year's sales, by using the average growth of the last couple of years during those months or even weeks. It all depends on that data that is available.

Different Ways That You Can Use Visual Basics for Applications

Like it was stated before, most programs don't have unique user-specific functions, like if a grocery store wanted to track its sales. Yeah, they could purchase a really expensive program that fits most of their needs, tracking sales and department shrink. But what if the manager wanted to compare data from one sheet to the next?

The data would have to be collected and placed on a different sheet. Then all the functions would have to be added just so that, that, data could be compared. Like if you wanted to compare last year's deli sales to this year's, or how many pounds of bananas were ordered for produce during February compared to July. You could even set up a competition between cashiers to see who gets the highest sale average per check out.

Review of Excel

Most Excel users are proficient in using the program, and this book unfolds the program's abilities even more. But, before we move on, let's review the more basic portions of Excel for those who are not that familiar with the properties of the program.

Excel is a program that provides the structure for multiple databases that can analyze and show information extrapolated from that data. Within Excel, there is something called object hierarchy, starting from the top is the program Excel. Which is followed by each file saved is a workbook, and you can add pages, also known as collections, for different objects, and each object can have different aspects. It is a kind of inception that can go even deeper but now isn't the time to go down that rabbit hole.

Please note that there are multiple ways for you to control and access functions in Excel. Unfortunately, not all of them will be covered.

Key Phrases and Punctuation Marks

Throughout this book will be many different terms, phrases, and punctuation marks that will not be familiar to all. Compiled below is a list of items that will appear in the coming chapters.

Array -	A group of variables.
Boolean -	A variable that holds the value of true or false.
Double -	A more specific variable than an integer that allows for the storage of decimals.
Else -	Follows an If Then statement, allowing for a second condition to be coded.
Events -	Coding that allows for a set of instructions to be activated when certain conditions are met (i.e. opening the file.)
If Then -	A statement in coding that when specific conditions are met it executes the code.
Integer -	A phrase that is used to store whole numbers (no decimals or letters).

Loop -	A shortened way of coding that allows you to go back to the beginning of your code and not have to type it repeatedly
Macro -	A chain reaction of one set of instructions triggering a secondary set of instructions (or more), that are used to complete a specific task.
Range -	Defines the specific cell that will be used in that code.
Spreadsheet -	A computer application that allows for the analysis and storage of data.
String -	Allows you to store text in coding.
Variable -	undefined terms/data shown in coding, in math it would be indicated with a letter (x).
Variables -	What is used to define the variable for the computer.
Workbook -	Collection of spreadsheets

The terms defined previously are just a few of the things that will be covered in this book. In addition to those, there will also be coding examples and some coding practice in chapter six. There will also be pictures that are to show what you should see written out and what some of the results of our coding should be.

Note: It is important to remember that even in the simplest lines of code that there could be errors and that debugging is part of the process. But we will show you how to go through the lines of code and see where the problem(s) are occurring. Yes, it took me a few tries with certain lines of code, and before I got the correct result, there was a bit of frustration, along with nonsense threats to the inanimate computer.

Now onto key punctuation marks that you will use while coding. Most of the punctuation marks you will recognize from regular everyday interactions. Others you will remember from math class and even some that you knew of but never knew the name of.

And they are as follows:

. Period	= Equal Sign
" " Quotation Marks	( ) Parenthesis
< Less than	> Greater than
& Ampersand	: Colon

All the punctuation marks listed above are used throughout all computer languages but do not necessarily the same meaning. The equal sign (=) in Visual Basics for Applications replaces whatever is on the left side of it for the right side, for example, and as we go along you will see that the punctuation marks will play an impact on your coding.

Chapter 2

Setting Excel up for Creating Visual Basics for Applications

How to Activate That Developer Tab

First, before we start coding, there is a step that needs to be completed in order for you to be able to use Macros and code. In the older versions, they have you go into your Excel program and open a new spreadsheet.

First, you need to select a cell and then right-click on the Ribbon. A drop box should appear, go down and select the option to customize the ribbon. The ribbon is the area where you can input data and formulas into the cell that you've selected.

A new dialog box should appear; in it, there should be a dropdown box underneath the phrase Customize Ribbon. Click the drop-down box and select the Main Tabs option.

That should make a clickable and expandable list for the Main Tabs. The one that you need to select and put a checkmark next to it is Developer if it isn't already activated. Once you've selected it, click the Okay button and there should be a new tab labeled Developer now at the top of the Excel program with all your other Main Tabs.

With some of the newer Excel programs, you don't need to go through your Ribbon in order to activate your Developer Tab. Newer versions do not show the customize ribbon option either. For the newer versions you do not need to make a new spreadsheet, in fact before you even open anything, over on the left-hand side is a list, at the very bottom of the list underneath Feedback is the Options button for the program, click that. A dialog box will pop up labeled Excel Options. On the left-hand side of this dialog box, most of the way down select the option labeled Customize Ribbon, select that option. This time on the right-hand side of the options window, the drop-down box from earlier should already have Main Tabs selected, and it should list all the Main Tabs that can appear when you open a spreadsheet or workbook. Going down that list Developer should be there, and you should select it. Now click okay, and you're set.

The picture before this paragraph is what the popped-up dialog box should look like either way. And the Result is the picture after this paragraph with an arrow pointing to your brand-new Developer tab on display.

An Explanation of Macros

Before we get into creating a code for a function, we need an explanation of Macros. Macro is short for macroinstruction; it's a condition that expands automatically into a secondary set of instructions that are then followed by the computer. This sounds like a lot, but the way it works is similar to clicking on a link on a website, now you've met the condition needed to activate the secondary set of instructions, which brings you to the page that you clicked on.

Going back to the top of the Excel screen, if you click on your developer tab, the top of the screen should show a new set of options. One of the options in the new tab should be inserted. The button looks like a toolbox with a wrench and screwdriver in front of it. Select insert and a drop-box should appear with different pictures of controls on it like displayed below.

In the dropdown tab, there are several options on it, we are going to focus on the Form Controls section, and on the top left of the little menu is the button command that we are going to be using throughout this book. Note: Unless otherwise specified, all the exercises and formulas will be using that button.

Macros, as stated before, are functions that the computer can perform when certain conditions are met but breaking down the process a little further will help some to understand how the coding for macros is written. Like when you break down the animal kingdom into classes and species and then scientific names, a macro breakdown goes like this:

Macros

⇧

Lines of code

⇧

Commands

Macros are made up of lines of code which contains the commands that you want the computer to perform. Commands encompass a host of things between the possible variables, ranges, text, and conditions that you want to be met. You can use those commands to create lines of code; some lines are long but, there is a way to make it more manageable, and it will be shown and described later. Finally, all those lines of code create macros, the function that you want the computer to perform. As you type up these Macros, save your progress as you go along. This process will allow you to, later on, recall those macros so that you will have a rough outline of functions that you can adjust to your own specifications.

Say if you were a teacher and you want to quickly see the average of all your students, you can open a spreadsheet and type up a macro that averages all the kids' individual grades and get the grade point average all at once. Think of the time saved once it is set up; it would be even easier to save the formula to use later and place on a blank spreadsheet. From there, you would be able to create a template that is easy to use for different subjects for students or for one subject with different classes of students.

We have gone over some of the basics of what Excel is capable of doing. We have also covered some of the terms that will be introduced later on in this book and have set up Excel to have a Developer tab.

Let's start learning more in-depth about macros and start coding.

Chapter 3

Creating your First Macro

Setting up a Basic Button Macro

Now that we are all set up to create Macros, this is where things get turned up a hair. Remember that little dropdown button on the Developer tab, the one that has a picture of a toolbox from earlier? Click it.

And select the plain rectangle on the left side of the dropdown tab, then on the spreadsheet below click anywhere on the right side of column F. This is to make sure that we will not place the button on the cells that we are going to be using for data during the rest of the book. The screen should look similar to the picture below.

Function vs. Sub

Adding a little clarification, there will be some vocabulary that will be similar, but again with the hierarchy, some of the words are on different levels. One of those examples is the words function and sub; they have similar meanings. The function is using code to achieve a result and sub, which is similar, as far as using a code, but the difference is that you do not receive a result from a sub. Sub is like right-clicking copy and paste, where a function is like entering an equation into a calculator and hitting enter.

Getting that Button to have a Function

Now, when you place the button, a new dialog box will appear the title on it is Assign Macro. On it should be a dropbox labeled Macro Name, there should not be anything in the drop-down box; there have not been any Macros created yet. Later, the more that gets coded and saved, there will be other options. For now, though select the new button, and a whole new window should pop up. The new window should be titled Microsoft Visual Basic for Applications-Book1. When you save this later, the title Book1 will change to whatever you want it to be. The computer or laptop screen should look like this now.

So the larger window in the background is where you are going to be performing all the magic of Visual Basic for Applications. All the coding is going to be placed on the lines in this box. Please note that most of the coding with that button will start with the phrase of Sub and end with, end sub, this tells the computer where the instructions start and ends. Whatever gets typed in between those two phrases will be considered code by the computer, and it will run through trying to follow the code until it hits a snag.

Now let us start with a little warm up, shall we? We are going to highlight a group of the cells with the button you just created and placed on the spreadsheet. The coding for this function goes like this:

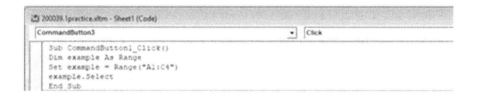

This coding shows as so when you click the button that you set up on the spreadsheet page. The result you should see is this:

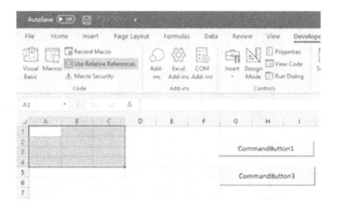

Congratulations if you got this on your first try (I most certainly did not). As you can see the cells between A1 and C4 are now highlighted. If you change your mind and want to highlight a row, you change the coding around a bit, so, say if you want to highlight row 3.

Go back to your coding screen and replace what was is written on line 3 with Example.Rows(3).Select

Dim example As Range

Set example = Range("A1:C4")

Example.Rows(3).Select

After finishing up head back to your spreadsheet, you can do this by clicking on the Excel screen, or there is a green Excel button up in the menu bar of the Visual Basic for Application at the top of the screen. Once back to your spreadsheet, click your CommandButton1 again.

You should have a highlighted Row 3 like it is shown.

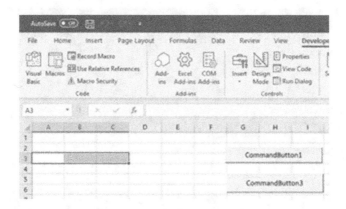

Now If you want to highlight a column replace the word Rows(3) with Columns(2) in your coding. This will lead you to highlight the second Column.

See, that was easy. Now you know how to highlight a Range, highlight a row or column within a Range of your choice. You can also highlight a cell by just placing its designation in the parentheses in the coding that we used to select the Range. Simple, right?

So far, we've set up a basic command button and have gotten that button to have a function. If you've had no problems with typing out the coding so far, that's GREAT! Now, for the wrench in the machine, as some call it.

Debugging

Debugging is something that will come up for anyone, and it usually occurs when you least expect it, but don't worry. We'll show you how to go through the code line by line to see where the computer does not understand just what it is you coded and what you want the computer to do.

Note: At some point during learning all this you will have to get up and walk away, I solemnly promise it was something that I had to do many times. Mostly due to that fact that the grammar in computer coding is different than that of regular English and I was putting a period instead of a comma.

Going back to that Visual Basic for Applications window type the following between the Sub and End Sub lines.

Dim example As Range

Set Ex =Range ("A1;C4")

Example.Select

Most of that coding is still the same as earlier, but there have been a few changes made. Can you see them? If you do not, there is a little play button up in the menu bar near the tabs. If you click it, the computer will pop out a message box saying what went wrong and even highlight where the computer is not able to read the coding. The programming version available to me corrected me before getting through typing all of the coding for the example.

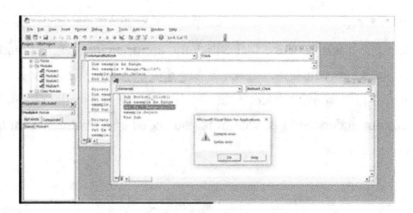

So now that we know the miscoding is in the second line, rewritten below, let us see what went wrong.

Set Ex = Range(A1;C4)

What the code should have been written as is this:

Set example = Range("A1:C4")

Did you get all that? The Ex should be an example. The A1:C4 should be in quotation marks and the punctuation mark between the two cells listed originally a semicolon and was changed to a colon. It is those little things that make the computer unable to read the code.

Computers are set up to understand certain phrases, and punctuation marks mean certain things, as stated at the beginning of this book.

So, let us take a look at some of the punctuation marks and what they usually mean in Visual Basic for Applications coding.

Colon :	Means between ex: ("A1:C4")
Equal Sign =	Designates the value for the variable/ replaces the value
Greater than >	Used in an If Then statement, it can implement a yes/no statement and can be combined with <.

Less than <	Used in an If Then statement, it can implement a yes/no statement and can be combined with >.
Parenthesis ( )	Used to hold parameters/area that is in the coding. Be it for where the computer is picking up data or if it is placing new data onto the spreadsheet.
Period .	Denotes the end of a common business-oriented language.
Quotation Marks " "	Used to denote a string directly written into the code. I.e., written text or an area on the spreadsheet.

Most of the punctuation marks above are used on a regular basis when you are coding with Visual Basics for Applications. Though there are more punctuation marks used in coding more complex things, these will get you started.

Note: It is important to remember to walk away from the computer when you are having a hard time, I solemnly swear that I had to walk away many a time before I performed one of the ultimate forms of frustration, the table flip. It wouldn't have been pretty, and I'd have lost a laptop.

Chapter 4

The Different Functions That Visual Basics for Applications Can Do

Starter Macros

For starter Macros, we will start with some of the basics. We will do:

A Message Box   Count

Current date and time   Clear

Copy and Paste   Count Rows/Columns

These choices were made to introduce you to some of the types of coding that you can perform in Visual Basic for Application. Later on, there will be harder coding.

The coding for most of the things above is usually about three lines of code. Think of a coded line as a sentence and all the lines put together as a paragraph that the computer reads like an instruction. To start off, we will count the number of boxes in the area that we highlighted earlier. It will make it easier since we already have most of that coding written out.

Counting

For this please type up:

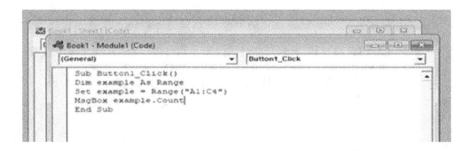

So, we have written for the computer to read the code and to count the number of cells between A1 and C4. The first line indicates that the area is called example and that we are going to be working with the indicated cells. The second line tells the computer where it is located, between A1 and C4. The third line says *MsgBox example.count* .

The term MsgBox stands for message box, and the computer is now being told to create a message box for the answer. Examples.count is the answer to the function that we want the computer to perform. If all goes well, there should be a message box on your screen stating that the counted number of cells is 12.

Counting Rows or Columns

The coding for the counting of Rows or Columns is essentially the same as the counting of the cells, but, the third line changes a bit.

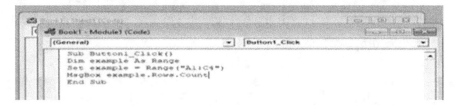

This time a message box should pop up and say that there are four rows in the selected area. You can then switch out the word Rows, for Columns. Say we change it to:

MsgBox example.Columns.Count

From that, you would get the number of Columns as well. For this line of coding the answer, you should get three.

Copy and Paste

Next, it's onto Copy and Paste. Have you ever needed to put in a repeated number for cells? Below, written down is the coding for copy and paste for any number of cells that you choose.

Before we start this new coding, go back onto your spreadsheet screen. Type in cell A1- Hello and in cell A2- There. This is going to be the data we are copying and pasting, now back to the coding screen and type in:

The first two lines of code above tell the computer what cells are selecting and that we are copying the data contained within the cells. The third line shows where we want to paste the copied data and the fourth line says to go ahead and paste it so your screen should now look like this:

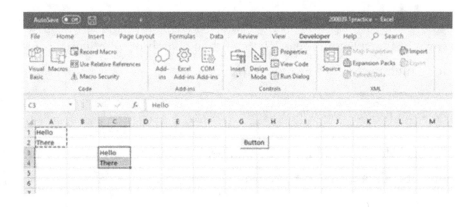

Pretty cool right?

Clearing the Cells

To now clear out these Cells, we will use a different code. You can do this two different ways, either by using a clear contents command or a value= "." Both still start out the same it just depends on your preference.

Range ("A1:C4").ClearContents

> Or

Range("A1:C4").Value=" "

These codes will empty all the cells within the A1-C4.

Message Box

Remember how when you were having the computer count the cells, and you had a message box pop up? Now we can code to have it say whatever we want it to. This code is just one line.

MsgBox "My name is (insert your name here)"

Simple. Easy, and now you have a message box telling you its name is the same as yours. We are going to show more of what the message boxes can do, but we will some of the more advanced capabilities later.

Getting the Date and Time

In order for you to receive the date and time in a message box. Type into the Visual Basic for Application screen:

MsgBox Now

Switch back over to the spreadsheet, hit that button and a box with that exact time and date will appear.

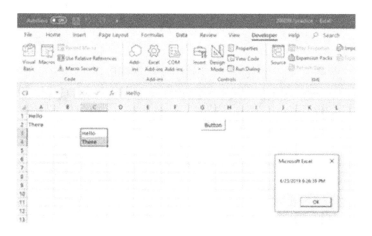

You can also get just the hour minute and second by altering the code a bit.

MsgBox Hour(now) – Hour

MsgBox Minute(Now) – Minute

MsgBox Second(Now) – Second

27

As a little added bonus Excel sees a 24 hour period of time as a whole number (1 actually) so if you enter the following code, you will see how far you are through a 24 hour period.

```
Sub Button1_Click()
Dim y As Double
y = TimeValue("09:20:01")
MsgBox y
End Sub
```

The response is a message box that tells you 0.388900462962963.

Variables

Variable- an element, feature, or factor that is liable to vary or change.

This is where things get a bit more complex. Below are a few different types of variables that have different functions, and they will be explained as we go along.

Integer	Double	String
If Then statement	Else statement	Boolean

Integer

Integers are used, to store whole numbers and only whole numbers. If you try to store a decimal or fraction, it will automatically round it up or down to the nearest whole number. Like the copy and paste that we used earlier to copy information from one cell to another, we can also place information in cells by using an integer code. The code following will allow you to place value in a selected cell.

28

In the first line above x is being defined as the integer. The second line states X is being replaced with 46. The last line of code names the cell A1 is where the value of x is located. If all the coding goes correctly in cell A1, a 46 should appear after you click your button.

Like it was stated before integers only store whole numbers. So, if we take the coding from above and place a decimal in 46 and change it to 4.6, instead of 4.6 being placed in cell A1, a 5 will appear because that is the closest whole number.

Double

The integer function holds whole numbers and the Double function holds decimals. By using the same formula that we used for the integer, we can replace the function integer and use double instead.

Same break down of the code lines as the other day. X is defined as double in the first line. In the second line, x is equal to 3.1415, and the last line contains the cell that x is supposed to go in. Click the little button, and you will see that cell A1 now has 3.1415 in it. Easy as pie, right?

String

It's now time to "string" things along (sorry for the pun). The variable string allows for the storing of text. So, say that we wanted to make a list of multimedia titles, you could easily type the title and what media it is so that the computer knows its title *and* what type of media. By taking the example of Grimm's' Fairytales by Jacob and Wilhelm Grimm, a book that has most of our childhood stories. In the picture below, the formula coded into the Visual Basic of Applications, below that is the result of our coding.

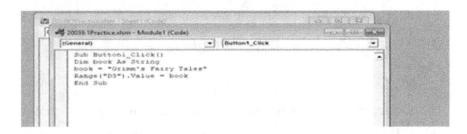

Starting with the top line that you have written, the computer is told that the book is going to be the variable. On the second line, the book is going to be assigned the value of 'Grimm's' Fairy Tales.' Lastly, the third line is telling the computer to that the in cell A1 is to have the value of book within it.

Resulting in:

When you code this way, you can add more data to a spreadsheet and not take up more room. It will allow you to, later on, separate it easier. Say you are making a chart of your friends' favorite entertainment, there are a couple of different categories, movies, books, sports, and games. You can just type in the title of their favorite thing and code into it that it's one of the things listed before.

Boolean

We have gone through the variables of integer, double and string, Boolean is next. Boolean is a command that gives values either true or false. Using Boolean in your coding allows you to assign a variable's value as fact or fiction.

```
Sub Button1_Click()
Dim continue As Boolean
continue = True
If contue = True Then MsgBox "If it fits it sits"
End Sub
```

If all goes well, you will have a message box stating "If it fits it sits."

If Then or Else

The following two types of variables are placed together because you can use If then, without Else, but you cannot use Else without If then. Quite a conundrum, right? If then is a conditional type of variable. Say, fictionally, if in a game you have 233 gold pieces and you want to use that gold for weaponry that's worth 175. When you go to purchase that, the fictional shopkeeper asks, "Hey, do you have enough gold pieces to cover the transaction for the weapon?" If the answer is yes you get the weapon; if the answer is no, then you're denied the weapon, citing that you don't have enough gold pieces to purchase the weapon. That is all that *if then* does, it places a condition that the cell that has to be met, in order to receive a coded response.

Moving forward with *If then*, place your cursor into A1 and type in a number between 0 and 100. Place a new command button and click new macro to go back to your Microsoft Visual Basic for Applications screen and enter the code:

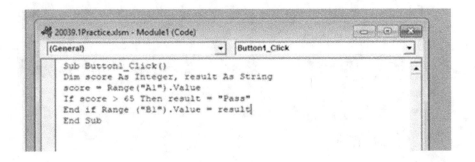

```
Sub Button1_Click()
Dim score As Integer, result As String
score = Range("A1").Value
If score > 65 Then result = "Pass"
End if Range ("B1").Value = result
End Sub
```

Starting from line one, we are placing score as the integer, and its location is going to be in A1. Also, in line one, we are telling the computer that there is going to be a second box that is going to be affected by the first part of the coding. Next, in line three, we are telling the computer that if the score is greater than (>) 60, the result is a pass. In line four, we are telling the computer that we want the result in B1.

Got it? Did you Pass? If you did not, that's okay because that means that B1 should be blank, so you passed even if B1 does not say so.

Else

This is where Else comes into play. Else, is a secondary condition that you can place in your coding/function to have a second result. Kind of like when you were a kid with a curfew of 10 if you got home in time you got a pass. But come home after 10 and you wind up grounded. *If then*, or *Else*.

Going back to your Visual Basic for Applications screen we are going to alter the previous coding a bit. We will also talk about how to break up code into smaller portions to make it easier for you to read.

```
20039.1Practice.xlsm - Module1 (Code)
(General)                              Button1_Click

Sub Button1_Click()
Dim score As Integer, result As String
score = Range("A1").Value
If score > 65 Then
    result = "Pass"
Else
    result = "Fail"
End If
    Range("B1").Value = result
End Sub
```

Above we have tabbed over to indent the typing of the coding, this technique is used to help in breaking up long lines of code into easier portions to read. It also lets us section off parts of the code that pertain to each other. Most of the code is the same as it previously was for *If then*, we only truly changed it up from line three.

As before lines one and two of the code places score as the integer and the location that it is going to be in and result as the string of stored text data. The third and fourth line above is the same as the third line from before, placing the condition that if the score is greater than 60, then its result is a "Pass." Now here is where things change up a bit because we have *Else* in line five, it places a second condition on the result. That condition is that if it does not meet the first condition, then it is listed as a "Fail." From there lines seven and eight tell the computer to place the answer to the coding into cell B1.

Again, did you pass, or did you fail? Either answer is actually a pass because you now have a working code.

Chapter 5

Longer Coding

The More You Learn the More You Code (Literally)

The snowball effect is about to happen; we have, so far, covered most of the basics to get a foundation. From here on out we are going to cover longer Macros and more in-depth ones. Over the previous chapters we have gone over the some of the different variables that can be used and the punctuations that go along with them, we still have a few more of each to go. But, don't worry, we are still going to be breaking down the examples and explaining what each step does. Remember that coding is a process and a language, so if it takes a bit to understand or get the hang of, then that's what it takes.

In this last chapter, before we set you up with different coding exercises and even some in depth question and answer, we are going to be covering quite a bit. We're going to be covering:

Loops   String Manipulation   Excel Events

Array(s)   ActiveX Controls   Application Object

Functions and Subs   Userform(s)

All of the things listed above will get harder and more in-depth as we go along, so like stated before, take your time. We will be going over everything that is coded and even shows what the process is in pictures.

Loops

Did you know that loops backward, is spool? Though we are not sewing here, we are stringing things together. Sorry, bad dad joke.

Loops are a type of coding that tells the computer to "thread" through a selected range of cells with just a few lines of code instead of having to repeat a code line multiple times. Beforehand, people had to write out all the lines of code in order to perform the same task. Also, there are single, double, and triple loops, and mind-blowingly there is a do-while loop. These four different loops allow you to work with dimensions.

What do I mean by dimensions? Dimensions that is being referenced is not the alternate reality that we see in all of the Marvel movies. Dimensions in Excel is a little simpler; it's the rows, columns, or filtering fields that we use to distinguish the data that we place on the worksheet. That doesn't mean the data that we actually enter into the cells; it is the labels on the x and y-axis that is used on a line graph.

Loop

Single loop coding allows you to go through one dimension of cells, and the coding goes like this:

```
20039.1Practice.xlsm - Module1 (Code)
(General)                              Button1_Click

Sub Button1_Click()
Dim i As Integer
For i = 1 To 6
Cells(i, 1).Value = 100
End Sub
```

When you have typed up this coding into the Visual Basic for Application screen, your result should be as shown:

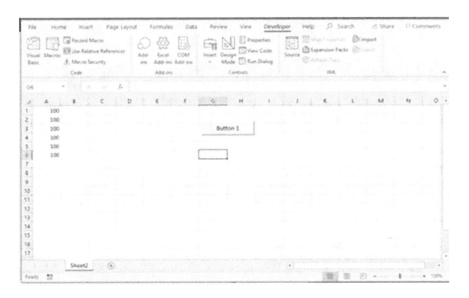

That's right you should have the number 100 in boxes one through six in column A. In line two it states that the value of (i) is to be executed six times and line three gives (i) the value of 100. In line three, there is also a one, that represents to start at Row one and Column One.

Double Loop

This explanation might not be as clear as it was with the single loop, the double might make it clearer as to how they placed it in Row 1, Column 1. The double loop allows you to go through two dimensions, and this might give you a better picture. The coding for this does expand a bit but not too complex. Ready?

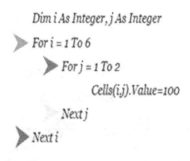

```
Dim i As Integer, j As Integer
    For i = 1 To 6
        For j = 1 To 2
            Cells(i,j).Value=100
        Next j
    Next i
```

Before going into the breakdown of what this coding does line by line, let's show you how it flows. We start from the top of the coding; the computer is going to read through the first four lines and then go down to the green arrow. This means that we have gone through and selected Row 1 and Column 1; reading the fourth line, the computer assigns the value of 100 to that cell. The processing system then goes back up to the red arrow because we are going from Column 1 to Column 2. From there the computer jumps down to the purple one. Once you get to the purple arrow, you go back up to the blue arrow and switch from Row 1 to Row 2. This process is repeated until all the Rows and Columns specified in the code are completed.

The coding gives us two variables i and j, i for Rows and j for Columns. To the right of them, the information given says how many times to execute the code, and the value of the cells is 100. Displayed are your results.

Ever wonder how a digital clock works without the second hand (like an analog clock) to tell it when sixty seconds are up? You guessed it, through programming, but not just any programming, through a loop. It works like this, the clock does not know when it needs to change the time, but the internal system has been programmed to count how many times that it needs to ask the question "Do I change the minute now?" Say that the inner processing unit is constantly asking this question, the inner computer knows that the processor had to ask that irritating question sixty times before it can say yes. Think of all those times that you repeatedly asked "Are we there yet?" Only the asking, again and again, does not stop.

Triple Loop

To place an emphasis on the fact that using a looping code permits you to abbreviate the coding necessary to perform what was just displayed. The start of the code would need at least four lines of code and for each of the additional five Rows that we want to fill would need two. That would make a minimum of 14 different lines of code that you would have to type up.

Up after the double loop is the triple loop, this looping coding not only allows for two dimensions but also has the ability to include other excel sheets. If you have any friends who own a business that deals with multiple running accounts, this is what you want to show them, or don't and ask them if they need a bookkeeper. With the triple loop, there is going to be quite a few variables, so before we start, we are going to shed some light on what some of the variables in the code are before explaining what is occurring within the code contains.

Before we start coding, you are going to be opening two new Worksheets; it will be necessary for you to have as the triple looping code coils its way through your three different spreadsheets. Yet again, create another command button and place it on your spreadsheet. Now for the code:

```
20039.1Practice.xlsm - Module1 (Code)
(General)                              ▼   Button1_Click

Sub Button1_Click()
Dim c As Integer, i As Inte  Object  j As Integer
For c = 1 To 3
    For i = 1 To 6
        For j = 1 To 2
            Worksheets(c).Cells(i, j).Value = 365
        Next j
    Next i
Next c

End Sub
```

Starting with the first integer c represents a worksheet, i represents the Rows and j represents the Columns.

The results of this coding should appear with three worksheets with the cells between A1 to B6 should be filled with 365.

If you've noticed that both the copy and paste function and the loop function have similar effects, you're right. Copy and paste repeats a cell's data to where you want it, and the loop places the data its code contains into the cells you want it. Either way, once you save your sheet your data can be altered and not have any effect on the other cells in the coding.

Do While Loop

Time to progress on to the Do While loop, a type of coding that is placed within a loop that is a condition that must be met in order for that line of code to be implemented on the spreadsheet, or else it remains inert or not activated for that loop of coding.

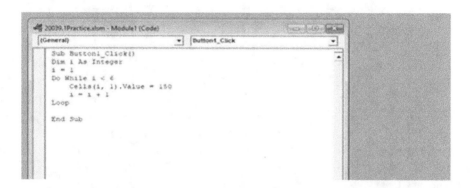

Above within the coding, the i is the variable and like in the previous representations of this type of coding i represents column A. In the second line i is replaced by 1; with the third line while i is less than 6 the value will equal 150. The fifth line is i=i+1 which is moving us down the column to Row 2, then there's the loop that brings us back up to the top of the whole coding, but i now is represented by 2.

Coding this correctly will result in you having Column A filled between Rows one through five filled with 150.

Switching it up a bit, pick six numbers and on a blank worksheet place them in Column A then setting up a new button for this page we are going to code:

Now if all goes well you will have Column B filled in with cell A's number plus 50, going down your column.

The Do While loop is fairly unique due to the fact that you can easily adjust all the cells that have writing in them again, it also does all the work for you. Adding 50 to all the cells is time-consuming, and nobody got time for that.

Before moving on, there was one point that I wanted to clarify, when you are using loop, each cell is going to be affected on its own. Whereas copy and paste, you are pasting to the range(s).

String Manipulation

In chapter four, we went over the basics of string equations, presently it is time to expand on what else we can do with Strings. From earlier we know that String is able to hold text information in coding, from here it's a lot of text manipulation that we are going to be coding.

First, by using the ampersand sign to "concatenate" or join two strings together. An ampersand is the "&" punctuation mark. For all of those who want the definition, it is a formal or technical term for linking things (objects) together in a series or chain. Like when you are going through a website, and you go from one page to another and another until you wind up back at the original page you didn't want.

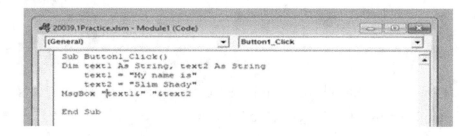

There is something new that we did with the punctuation marks in this coding. Can you tell what it is? If you take a look at the last line, there is a set of quotation marks that go around nothing, but that isn't quite what is happening. The quotation marks are being used to place a space in the sentence that we made so that it isn't all one string of letters.

Conclusively, the result of your coding should have resulted in a message box saying that its name is Slim Shady.

Manipulation

The manipulation of a text string is easy with some of the codes and more complex with others. You can manipulate the text a couple of different ways, from the right, left, or center; there is also length and instr.

Length

Length measures how many positions are within the string that you wrote. Positions meaning every keystroke between the two quotation marks in the code. So, if you write "I am Jam," the length of that sentence is 8. In between the quotation marks, there are eight keystrokes, "I•am•Jam." To measure the length of your text you are going to need this code.

Once you enter that text and click the command button your result will be 8, as stated earlier.

InStr

InStr is a syntax word that the computer recognizes as coding and is conceptually a shorter version of "in string". InStr allows you to start in a secondary position in the original string. It is often a little difficult to wrap your head around something that you have never seen before, but we will illuminate the functions process.

```
20039.1Practice.xlsm - Module1 (Code)
(General)                          Button1_Click
    Sub Button1_Click()
    Dim text As String
    text = "Starting Line"
    MsgBox Inst("Starting Line", "tart")
    End Sub
```

Right above is the function InStr, it runs just the same as length, just it has a different instruction. Lines one through three are the same as before only line four not only has an InStr, it also has two phrases inside of the parenthesis. Those are "Starting Line" and "tart," what we are asking the computer for is to look for "tart" within the phrase "starting line" and to tell us what position it starts in. If all went well, your result should reveal that the answer is 2.

Right

Manipulation of text is all about the positioning of the letters, for the next couple of codes, we are going to stick with "Starting Line" as the phrase used. Now everyone reads from left to right but to make this stick a bit better we will go from the right to left for starters. Ever forget to grab something, and you know that you forgot it but cannot remember what it was, instead of looking left to right (like when you read) look right to left, the change in habit will jog your brain into recognizing what you forgot.

The way that this coding works is it allows a specified number of positions from the right side to be shown.

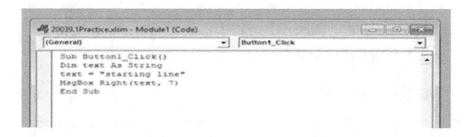

The result would be "ng line," because starting from the right side and counting seven positions in lands on the g in starting.

Left

This manipulation should be a bit easier because usually text is read left to right.

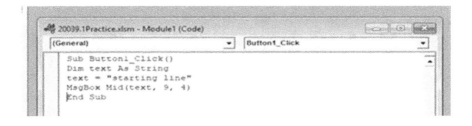

```
20039.1Practice.xlsm - Module1 (Code)
(General)                          Button1_Click

    Sub Button1_Click()
    Dim text As String
    text = "starting line"
    MsgBox = Left(text, 5)
    End Sub
```

This time around, we are starting from the left and counting 5 positions in; the result that we should receive is ***start***.

Mid

Mid, short for middle means exactly how it sounds, you start in the middle of the string. Though to be fair you do not have to start directly in the center of the string, you can start closer to either side; it just depends on your starting position. It also depends on how many positions you want to count over as well. To clear this up a bit:

```
20039.1Practice.xlsm - Module1 (Code)
(General)                          Button1_Click

    Sub Button1_Click()
    Dim text As String
    text = "starting line"
    MsgBox Mid(text, 9, 4)
    End Sub
```

Just like the right and left string, coding from before the first two lines are the same and the third one varies. In this one, the function starts you from a position in the middle of the string, which has been identified in the line as nine. The four, tells us how many positions that we are going over from the starting position.

The result that you should have gotten was "nest." We started off at position nine, which puts us at the i in line, here comes the somewhat tricky part. Because we started at position nine that becomes the beginning and everything else follows. Shown as "nestarting li," as you can see, we started from position nine and then "wrap around" until we get back to where position nine started.

Array

In computer tech terms an array is an assembly of variables. Remember how at the end of chapter 2 where there was an object hierarchy demo-ed? We are now going back to it and to just make an easy example the category of music is going to be used while we are making our way through the array.

1 Dimension Array

The word dimension denotes just one aspect of whatever subject you choose. As we stated earlier, the example that was chosen was Music. Let's start.

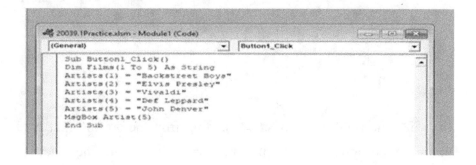

When you click away at your command button when you are all done coding, your answer will be presented in a message box. The Answer? John Denver.

2 Dimension Array

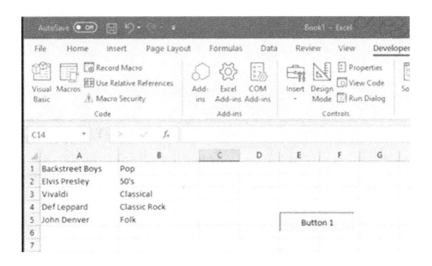

Stated before was that in Excel that dimensions are properties/character of an object, what was chosen was music. In the picture displayed is the music artists along with their genres.

```
20039.1Practice.xlsm - Module1 (Code)
(General)                                      Button1_Click

Sub Button1_Click()
Dim Music(1 To 5, 1 To 2) As String
Dim i As Integer, j As Integer
      For i = 1 To 5
      For j = 1 To 2
            Music(i, j) = Cells(i, j).Value
      Next j
      Next i
MsgBox Music(4, 2)

End Sub
```

In the picture, we have filled in the artists from before and the genres that they usually perform in. Those two characteristics form the two dimensions that are needed for the next function.

The coding above names the range and says that the data being used is text (String). At the end of the code, it asks for the information in Row 4, Column 2. Displayed is the answer that Excel gave me.

Note: Whenever you list the range without direct cell names, Rows are first, and Columns are second.

Events

Events are when users activate codes to perform actions, like when you turn on your computer, and it sounds like it's greeting you.

Workbook Open Event

In this part, you are not going to need a command button just the Visual Basics for Applications screen. On the left-hand side, there is a menu called project explorer with your workbook's name and the pages it contains listed below. In the picture, it shows the red arrow pointing to the menu, double click on the workbook. There should be a new window labeled Book1- This Workbook, and it should be blank, but we are going to type in:

MsgBox "Welcome Back"

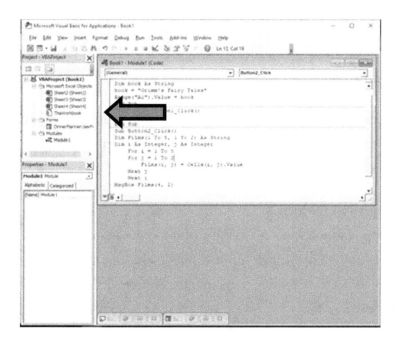

That way, we can save and close the file. Once the file is closed and you reopen it, you should receive a greeting from your workbook.

Worksheet Change Event

This enables you to have a window to pop up if you change a cell's value on a worksheet. An example is if you are trying to meet a sales goal and you finally beat it.

Using the same screen and menu as before with the Visual Basics for Applications editor double click on one of your worksheets, the coding window for that sheet will appear, and there are two drop boxes on the top of that window, select the one on the left and choose Worksheet. In the right-hand side drop-down list and select change. Next, you need to code:

If Target.Address = "D5" Then

If Target.Value > 150 Then MsgBox "You've reached your Donation goal."

The above coding states that the cell that is going to change is D5 and that if the value of that cell becomes more than 150, the result is you get a message stating that you have reached your goal.

Application Object

An application object allows for you to access options that are not readily available through the tabs, this includes screen updates when you place worksheet functions into the Ribbon and hold off on doing a calculation until you have finished placing your calculations in for that cell or for the whole page.

Screen Updating

This will allow you to put a pause on the screen updating until you are ready or if you want to have your computer run faster while it's not constantly updating the screen the whole time. It's very useful for when you are changing information on one part, and it has to update on another portion as well.

Using a regular command button Code in

This coding will allow you to slow down your screen, updating to a rate that you can see the coding taking place. And though this would be fascinating to keep on, you can also adjust the speed by removing a zero or two from the 10000. But sometimes there are time constraints, and we do not have the time to spend watching the coding taking effect, so, to take it off we code:

This will set your screen updating rate back to normal, so you do not have to wait for the computer to play through all the updates that you have placed or the command buttons that you have coded to take forever to complete a task.

Calculation

In addition to being able to slow the computers update screen, you can also put a pin in the computer calculating as you go along. You can actually manually do the calculations on your own by using the

F9 button on your keyboard. To stop the calculations from the computer you need a command button and to code:

Application.Calculation=xlCalculationManual

You can make sure that this went into effect by going through Files to options and then formulas. It should say that the calculations are manual now.

ActiveX Controls

ActiveX Controls are very similar to Form controls, only they allow for a more flexible coding. The following coding shows some of the different options that you can achieve with ActiveX controls.

Change Color of Font in a Range

Select the ActiveX command button from the drop-down menu; then right-click the button and click on the View Code option. You will notice that the coding of this is a little bit different from the Form button coding that we have previously used, instead of Sub it will say Private Sub. Code this into the box:

Selection.Font.Color=vbBlue

Once you've completed typing switch back to the excel spreadsheet and click on the button. All of the typing that you had on that spreadsheet previously will now be a blue color.

Userform

What's a Userform? Userforms are a custom dialog box that you can create through Visual Basics for Applications editor. Think of it as one of those forms you have to fill out if you are signing up for something, like a softball league. It allows you to have an infinite amount of options in creating it and what to put on it.

Please, take your time with this. It is the last thing that we are going to be showing how to create, and it is the most in-depth process that is going to be shown.

So now we go directly to the Visual Basics for Applications screen, click on view project explorer then go down to insert, and the option that you want to click is Userform. A toolbox should appear automatically if not there's a button on your menu bar that has a wrench and hammer, that will pop up a toolbox that will have your controls on it.

Within the toolbox, the controls allow us to design the Userform. Contained in the toolbox is the cursor, label, text box, combo box, list box, checkbox, option button, toggle button, frame, command button, Tab strip, Multipage, scroll bar, spin button, image and reference edit. Each has a different function but you have used or seen all the tools in that toolbox.

Now to list all the Objects that you will place on the Userform. Listed below are the objects that you will need. You can add all the objects at one time and then run through changing all the names or change them as you go along.

To change the name of the objects in the Userform, you click on an object that you have placed, then to the left and below the project-VBAproject, there should be a tiny window below that is labeled Properties. Within that window, you can change the name of the object, instead of keeping it as Textbox4 (for the fourth imaginary textbox that you have placed). You can do this for all of the objects that are on the list below.

Note: the VBAProject section contains all the worksheets, workbook and anything else that we have created within the project that you have been working on.

Object	Name for the computer	What the users see
Userform1	AdoptionSurvey	Adoption Survey
TextBox1	NameText	Name:
TextBox2	PhoneText	Phone:
ListBox1	TypeofList	Type of Pet
Frame	ExerciseLv	Exercise Level
CheckBox1	CouchCheck	Couch Potato
CheckBox2	ModCheck	Moderate
CheckBox3	CrossCheck	Cross Fit
OptionButton1	IOwnButton	I own my home
OptionButton2	RentButton	I rent my home
OptionButton3	OthersButton	I live with others.
CommandButton1	CancelB	Cancel
CommandButton2	ClearB	Clear
CommandButton3	ApplyB	Apply

In addition, please use the label option to label your Name and Phone number text boxes.

After you complete placing everything on your form, it should look a little like the picture shown. If it doesn't look perfect, that's okay because you probably won't be showing this to anybody anyway.

Next up is the Coding, so starting with going back to the Excel spreadsheet that we will place an ActiveX Command button and code it with:

AdoptionSurveyUserForm.Show

This is so that when we click on the button, it leads us to the user form that we are creating. Next up is back to the Visual Basics for Applications screen and going over to the left-hand side again and right-clicking on the AdoptionSurvey form that we created and renamed. Once the coding window appears, at the top there are two drop-down lists, in the right on select User Form and in the left select Initialize.

This is the part that I mentioned earlier. *Take. Your. Time.* This is the part that will be the most intensive in coding, and all the parts need to be right in order for the user form to work.

Everything coded for the User Form must be copied exactly, the Visual Basics for Applications program will tell you when something is wrong with the coding. It, however, will not tell you if your coding is sending the information to the wrong place or if it leads to nowhere.

We are going to activate the command buttons that we placed on the form now. This will take all the information that was collected in by the user form and place it on the spreadsheet. So, before we start with activating the command buttons switch over to the spreadsheet for a second and click on A1. Going across the row in separate boxes add the following: Name, Phone, Type, I live with and

Exercise level. Make sure you placed your command button from earlier is placed outside the area of the columns that you filled just filled in.

Jump back over to the Visual Basic for Application screen, the user form that we created should be in the most recent window. Select the Apply button with a double click. What follows is the coding will allow for all the information taken in by your form to be placed in the columns that we just labeled.

```
Sub Button1_Click()
Dim emptyRow As Long
'Make Sheet1 active
Sheet1.Activate
'Determine emptyRow
emptyRow = WorksheetFunction.CountA(Range("A:A")) + 1
'Transffer information
Cells(emptyRow, 1).Value = NameText.Value
Cells(emptyRow, 2).Value = PhoneText.Value
Cells(emptyRow, 3).Value = TypeofList.Value

If CouchCheck.Value = True Then Cells(emptyRow, 5).Value = CouchCheckCaption
If ModCheck.Value = True Then Cells(emptyRow, 5).Value = Cells(emptyRow, 5).Valu
If CrossCheck.Value = True Then Cells(emptyRow, 5).Value = Cells(emptyRow, 5).Va
If IOwnButton.Value = True Then
    Cells(emptyRow, 4).Value = "Own"
Else
    Cells(emptyRow, 4).Value = " "
End If
If RentButton.Value = True Then
    Cells(emptyRow, 4).Value = "Rent"
Else
    Cells(emptyRow, 4).Value = " "
End If
If OthersButton.Value = True Then
    Cells(emptyRow, 4).Value = "Other"
Else
    Cells(emptyRow, 4).Value = " "
End If

End Sub
```

Next up is the Clear button, so, double click on the Clear button and when the coding window pops up type in:

Call UserForm_Initialize

This is so when you click on it clears the whole form, without having to completely exit the Adoption Survey pop-up.

Next is the Cancel button, so if someone does not want to fill out the information or changed their mind and you only need to type in one line.

Unload Me

Got it all? Great! Now it's time to test your survey form. Go back to the Excel spreadsheet and click that button. Your Adoption user form should show up, and you can fill it out, I fill mine with fictional people to give an example. Check it out.

First up is how the form should look when you are all done and want to take in data.

Pretty neat, huh? We have almost everything that would be needed by an adoption group to consider what it would be possible for someone to adopt a pet.

Listed below here is the results of the fictional people entering their criteria for us to analyze. Like I said previously it doesn't matter if it doesn't look pretty, it just needs to work correctly.

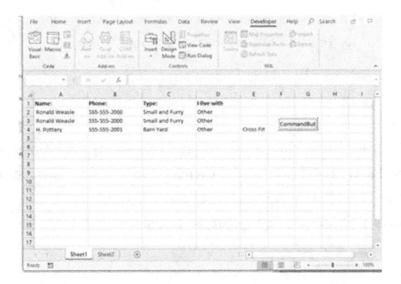

As you have now read through the book, let's get some more practice in so that we can solidify some of that knowledge and get some experience outside of the copying that you have been doing.

Chapter 6

Practice

Reviewing

For this chapter, we are going to go through some of the earlier works, and at the end, I will be writing the coding that you will need to have in order to get the results intended. There's a couple of different practices that will be given to you, some of the coding that we covered will be wrong and see if you can correct it. There will also be fill in blanks or correct the coding, along with coding written out that you will have to say what is the result.

1. What is the result of the coding?

```
20039.1Practice.xlsm - Module1 (Code)

(General)                              Button1_Click

    Sub Button1_Click()
    Dim x As Integer
    x = 8.9
    Range ("A1")

    End Sub
```

2. What kind of Visual Basic for Applications coding is this?

```
20039.1Practice.xlsm - Module1 (Code)
(General)                          Button1_Click

Sub Button1_Click()
Dim continue As Boolean
continue = True
If contue = True Then MsgBox "If it fits it sits"
End Sub
```

3. If a Visual Basic coding assigned a value of True or False, What, is the term for this type of coding?

4. If I want the Workbook that I'm working on to remind me to update the totals every Monday, Wednesday, and Friday, and to Call all the Customers that are delinquent on payments. What is the name of what I want to happen, and how would I code it?

5. What is my result?

```
20039.1Practice.xlsm - Module1 (Code)
(General)                          Button1_Click

Sub Button1_Click()
Dim text As String
text = "Table and Chairs"
MsgBox Right(text, 7)
End Sub
```

6. How many cells have been filled in with 155? What type of Loop is this called?

```
20039.1Practice.xlsm - Module1 (Code)
(General)                              Button1_Click

Sub Button1_Click()
Dim c As Integer, i As Integer, j As Integer
    For c = 1 To 3
    For i = 1 To 7
    For j = 1 To 4
        Worksheets(c).Cells(i, j).Value = 155
    Next j
    Next i
    Next c
End Sub
```

7. If someone wanted to place a decimal into a code, what type of variable would be needed to do so?

a. Integer   b. String   c. Boolean   d. Double

8. How many cells would be highlighted in this code?

```
20039.1Practice.xlsm - Module1 (Code)
(General)                              Button1_Click

Sub Button1_Click()
Dim example As Range
Set example = Range("A2:F6")
MsgBox example.Count
End Sub
```

9. What portion of this coding belongs to the user form that we created earlier?

```
20039.1Practice.xlsm - Module1 (Code)
(General)                              Button1_Click

Sub Button1_Click()
'Empty TypeofList
'Fill TypeofList
With TypeofList
    .AddItem "Dog"
    .AddItem "Cat"
    .AddItem "Pig"
    .AddItem "Small and Furry"
    .AddItem "Barn Yard"
End Sub
```

10. What is the difference between an ActiveX control and a Form Control?

11. What is the code that you would use in order to get that moment's Date and Time?

12. How does Excel see time, and what is the result if you put the previous question's answer is put into that form?

Please use the spreadsheet provided to answers for 13 and 14

13. What would the result be?

```
20039.1Practice.xlsm - Module1 (Code)
(General)                          Button1_Click

Sub Button1_Click()
Dim films(1 To 5, 1 To 2) As String
Dim i As Integer, j As Integer
    For i = 1 To 5
    For j = 1 To 2
        films(i, j) = Cells(i, j).Value
End Sub
```

14. What would the result be?

```
20039.1Practice.xlsm - Module1 (Code)

(General)                                    Button1_Click

Sub Button1_Click()
Dim films(1 To 5, 1 To 2) As String
Dim i As Integer, j As Integer
    For i = 1 To 5
    For j = 1 To 2
        films(i, j) = Cells(i, j).Value
    Next j
    Next i
MsgBox films(7, 1)
End Sub
```

1. What is the result?

```
20039.1Practice.xlsm - Module1 (Code)
(General)                    Button1_Click

Sub Button1_Click()
Dim x As Integer
x = 8.9
Range ("A1")

End Sub
```

The result from this was a little tricky but, if you remember from the beginning that Integers only hold whole numbers then you should be good

Result= 9

2. What kind of Visual Basic for Applications coding is this?

```
20039.1Practice.xlsm - Module1 (Code)
(General)                    Button1_Click

Sub Button1_Click()
Dim text As String
text = "starting line"
MsgBox Right(text, 7)
End Sub
```

Answer: The name for this type of coding is If then. We used this to tell us if you "Passed"

3. If a Visual Basic coding assigned a value of True or False, What, is the term for this type of coding?

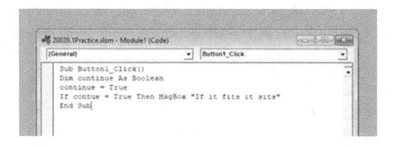

Answer: Boolean is the type of coding that you can assign a true or false value to.

4. I want the Workbook that I'm working on to remind me to update the totals every Monday, Wednesday, and Friday, and to Call all the Customers that are delinquent on payments. What is the name of what I want to happen, and how would I code it?

Answer: Type of coding is called an event.

How to code this:

Go into the Visual Basics for Applications and double click the workbook that you want to remind you and code in:

MsgBox "Update accounts every Monday, Wednesday, and Friday. Also, call delinquent customers on the same days."

5. What is my result?

```
20039.1Practice.xlsm - Module1 (Code)
(General)                              Button1_Click

Sub Button1_Click()
Dim text As String
text = "starting line"
MsgBox Mid(text, 9, 4)
End Sub
```

Result: _Chairs

6. How many cells have been filled in with 155? What type of Loop
   is this called?

```
20039.1Practice.xlsm - Module1 (Code)
(General)                              Button1_Click

Sub Button1_Click()
Dim c As Integer, i As Integer, j As Integer
    For c = 1 To 3
    For i = 1 To 7
    For j = 1 To 4
        Worksheets(c).Cells(i, j).Value = 155
    Next j
    Next i
    Next c
End Sub
```

Answer: 63 Cells should be filled with the number 155. The term for
   this loop is a Triple loop.

7. If someone wanted to place a decimal into a code, what type of variable would be needed to do so?

   a. Integer   b. String   c. Boolean   d. Double

Answer: Double.

   Integers store whole numbers

   String stores text

   Boolean is to assign a true or false value to a variable

   Double allows you to store numbers other than whole

8. How many cells are highlighted in this code?

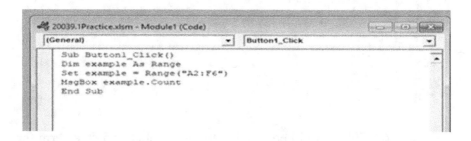

Answer: 30 cells Five cells down and six cells across 5*6=30

9. What portion of this coding belongs to the user form that we created earlier?

```
20039.1Practice.xlsm - Module1 (Code)

(General)                               Button1_Click

    Sub Button1_Click()
    'Empty TypeofList
    'Fill TypeofList
    With TypeofList
         .AddItem "Dog"
         .AddItem "Cat"
         .AddItem "Pig"
         .AddItem "Small and Furry"
         .AddItem "Barn Yard"
    End Sub
```

Answer: This portion of the code belongs to the list box that we could select the type of pet that we chose.

10. What is the difference between an ActiveX control and a Form Control?

The difference between an ActiveX control and Form Control is that form control follows a set of codes that are already programmed into the computer. Whereas, ActiveX controls allow for a more flexible and customizable coding that allows you to create your own code when needed.

11. What coding would you use to get this moment's date and time?

Answer: *MsgBox Now*

12. How does Excel see time, and what is the result if you put the previous question's answer is put into that form?

Answer: Excel sees time as an integer. The time was placed in as the variable

Please use the spreadsheet provided to answers for 13 and 14

13. What would the result be?

```
20039.1Practice.xlsm - Module1 (Code)

(General)                          Button1_Click

Sub Button1_Click()
Dim films(1 To 5, 1 To 2) As String
Dim i As Integer, j As Integer
    For i = 1 To 5
    For j = 1 To 2
        films(i, j) = Cells(i, j).Value
    Next j
    Next i
MsgBox films(3, 2)
End Sub
```

Answer: Leonardo DiCaprio

14. What would the result be?

```
20039.1Practice.xlsm - Module1 (Code)

(General)                              Button1_Click

Sub Button1_Click()
Dim films(1 To 5, 1 To 2) As String
Dim i As Integer, j As Integer
    For i = 1 To 5
    For j = 1 To 2
        films(i, j) = Cells(i, j).Value
    Next j
    Next i
MsgBox films(7, 1)
End Sub
```

Answer: Knocked Up

There are more examples and different codes that you can practice with available online. Listed below are some of the different websites that will give you practice with Visual Basics for Applications coding.

Reminder/Disclaimer: This book is not affiliated with any of these websites or has any claim to them and listed websites did not endorse to be placed here.

Excel Easy- this website holds a lot of information and offers around 300 different examples on it and covers basics too.

https://www.excel-easy.com/

Code VBA – another website that offers tons of information; it also offers a list of the functions that are already programmed into Excel and what they are capable of.

http://codevba.com/

The photos, in the beginning, were collaged together but they were obtained from:

Computer History- Computerhistory.org

Wikipedia- En.wikipedia.org – under Floppy Disk

All other photos were created for this book.

Conclusion

I want to congratulate all of the people who made it through until the end. You now have a firm grasp on Visual Basics for Applications. I especially want to congratulate those who had to get up from their computer a time or two because this is not as easy of a task as the movies and TV shows would like for us to think that it is (though there are those out there that can do that).

Many thanks for downloading and reading this book!

I am hoping that this book was able to help you to add to the intensification your knowledge of computer programs and to have added an extra skillset that you never knew that you could do. I also hope that it helps you to give you confidence in even more than just about Visual Basics for Applications and for you to go beyond just this.

The next step is to keep practicing on your own so that your skills never get rusty and so that you can improve over time. You never know you might just impress the right person and get a great job offer.

Finally, I'd like to ask for a gargantuan favor of you. Please head over to Amazon.com and review the book. Remember the more you liked it, the better the review (just kidding). I'd appreciate any feedback and suggestions that you have.

Once again, thank you for reading, and I hope everyone keeps learning.

www.ingramcontent.com/pod-product-compliance
Lightning Source LLC
La Vergne TN
LVHW051747050326
832903LV00029B/2776